C0-BWZ-713

What Do I Use?

Kate McGough

ETA
Cuisenaire

I am a chef.
I cook food.

What do I use?

I am a **gardener**.
I take care of plants.

What do I use?

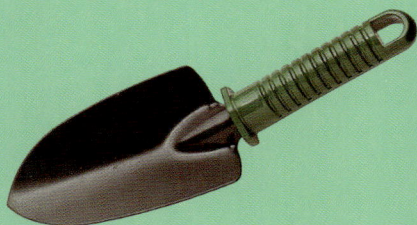

5

I am a **carpenter**.
I build houses.

What do I use?

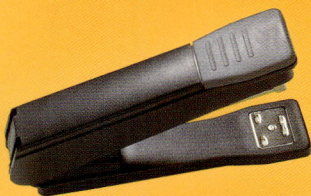

I am a **doctor**.
I help sick people.

What do I use?

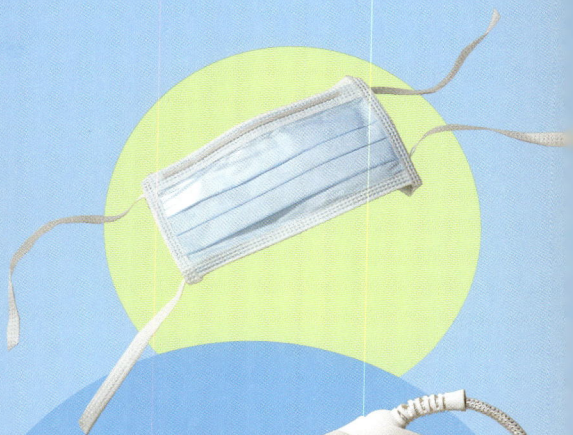

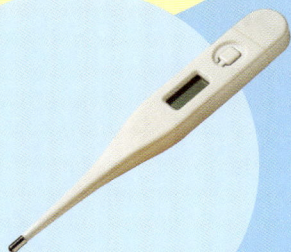

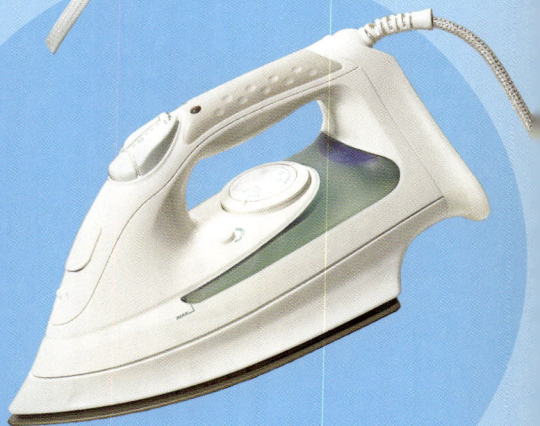

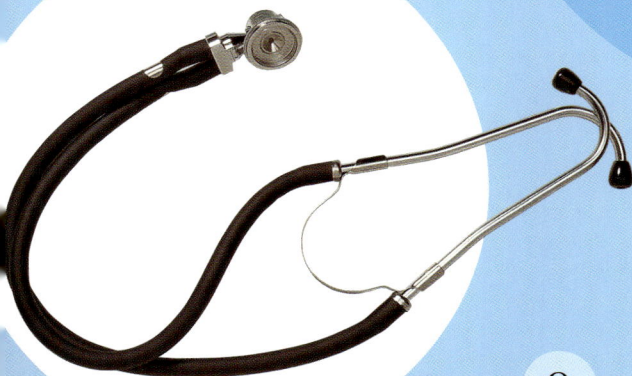

I am a **photographer**.
I take photographs.

What do I use?

Did you find the things the people use?

chef

rolling pin

mixing bowl

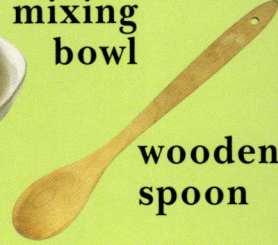

wooden spoon

gardener

trowel

watering can

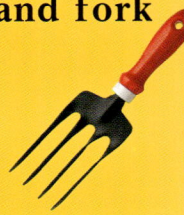

hand fork

carpenter

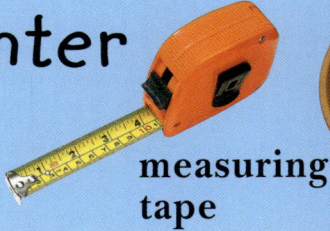

measuring tape

nails

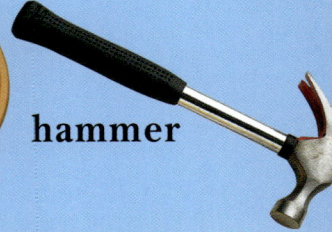

hammer

doctor

thermometer

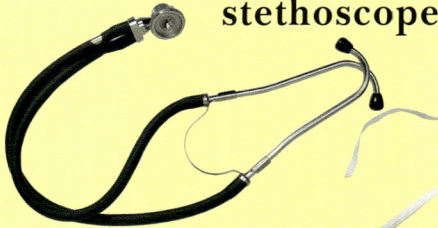

stethoscope

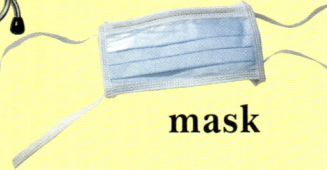

mask

photographer

film

flash

camera